貝多芬

Heroes and Role Models | Non-Fiction Series

Copyright © 2022 by Level Learning, INC. and Washington Yu Ying PCS™
Original and Edited Text Copyright © 2022 by Washington Yu Ying PCS™

All rights reserved. No part of this book in whole or part may be reproduced without written permission from the publisher.

Published by Level Learning, INC.

Content Contributors:
Washington Yu Ying PCS™
Level Learning - Ya-Ching Chang

Illustrations by: Josh Taira

Leveling classification based on Level Learning standard. For full description, visit www.levellearning.com

ISBN 978-1-64040-045-0
Traditional Chinese Edition

About Level Learning:
Level Learning provides a literacy focused curriculum specifically designed for K-12 Chinese as a Second Language classrooms. Our program offers 20 levels of specific and detailed objectives, leveled texts and passages, mastery-based online assessment, and analytics to enable data-driven instruction. Level Learning reading curriculum for both literature and informational text emphasize grammar and comprehension skills to help teachers develop confident and independent Chinese language readers. The non-fiction series of books are specifically designed to support our informational text course based on multiple national standards. To learn more about our entire offering, visit www.levellearning.com.

About Washington Yu Ying PCS™:
Washington Yu Ying PCS is a Mandarin English dual language immersion International Baccalaureate (IB) World school. Yu Ying's mission is to inspire and prepare young people to create a better world by challenging them to reach their full potential in a nurturing Chinese/English educational environment. Yu Ying's comprehensive IB, dual immersion curriculum equips students with global competencies for success in the real world. As a leader in immersion education, Yu Ying is determined to advance Chinese language programs and global citizenry education by helping other schools create and strengthen their Chinese programs. For more information, email: products@washingtonyuying.org

貝多芬生於1770年。他是在德國出生的。

貝多芬的爺爺和爸爸都是音樂家。因此，他小時候就常常和爸爸學習音樂。

貝多芬非常喜歡音樂。他也<u>進步</u>得非常快。

貝多芬小時候就常常參加音樂表演。大家都很喜歡他的表演。

長大以後，貝多芬到維也納學習音樂。在那裡，有許多有名的音樂家。

在維也納，貝多芬經常參加音樂表演。他也學習**作曲**。

可是後來,貝多芬的耳朵聽不清楚了。慢慢地,他聽不見聲音,也聽不見音樂了。

雖然聽不見，貝多芬還是努力地作曲。

貝多芬寫了九首有名的交響曲。他也成為了一位有名的作曲家。

Glossary

	Pinyin	English Definition
德國	dé guó	Germany
出生	chū shēng	born
音樂家	yīn yuè jiā	musician
學習	xué xí	to learn
音樂	yīn yuè	music
進步	jìn bù	to improve
參加	cān jiā	to participate
表演	biǎo yǎn	performance
維也納	wéi yě nà	Vienna
有名	yǒu míng	famous
作曲	zuò qǔ	to compose
聽	tīng	to listen, to hear
清楚	qīng chu	clear
聲音	shēng yīn	sound
努力	nǔ lì	work hard
交響曲	jiāo xiǎng qǔ	symphony

www.ingramcontent.com/pod-product-compliance
Lightning Source LLC
Chambersburg PA
CBHW041223070526
44584CB00001B/76